What Is
THE MOON?

I LIKE SPACE!

Carmen Bredeson

WORDS TO KNOW

astronaut (AS truh not)
A person who works in outer space.

gravity (GRA vih tee)
The force that pulls things toward each other. When you jump up, Earth's gravity pulls you back down to the ground.

lava (LAH vuh)
Melted rock that comes out of a volcano.

reflect (rih FLEKT)
To turn back light; to bounce light off something.

CONTENTS

What is the Moon?

The Moon is a giant rock that goes around Earth. Scientists believe that it used to be part of Earth.

Fun Fact

The Moon looks mostly gray. A layer of dust hides orange dirt, green rocks, and maybe other colorful things!

Where did the Moon come from?

Earth

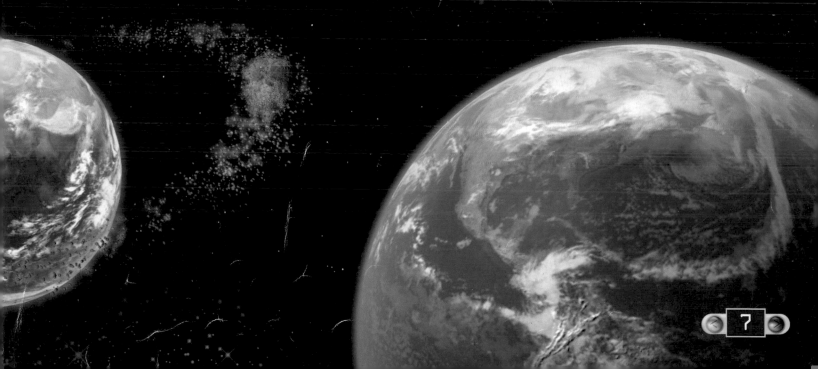

Scientists think that, long ago, a giant space rock crashed into Earth. Melted rock splashed far out into space. It made a ring that went around and around Earth. Part of the ring formed a ball and turned into the Moon.

Moon

How big is the Moon?

Pretend that you cut Earth into four pieces and rolled the pieces into giant balls. Each ball is the same size. The Moon would be the size of one of the balls.

Fun Fact

Mount Everest is the highest mountain on Earth. Some mountains on the Moon are taller than Mount Everest.

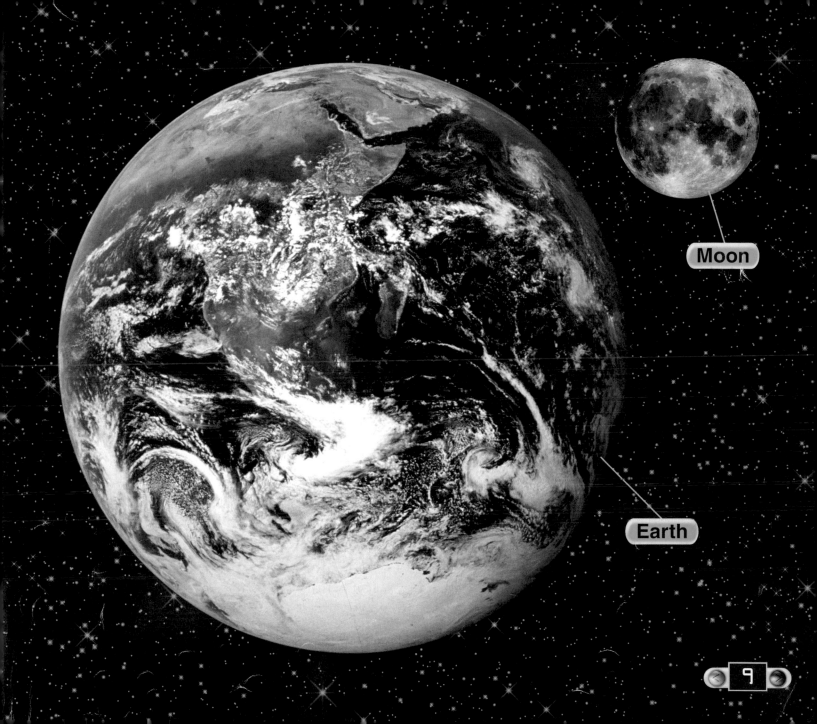

Moon

Earth

What makes the Moon shine?

Light from the Sun shines on the Moon. The Moon reflects the light like a big mirror. The Moon does not make its own light like the Sun does.

Fun Fact

It is very cold in the shade and at night on the Moon. If you dropped a rubber band it would break into many pieces because it would be frozen.

Yes. Every four weeks, the Moon makes one trip around Earth. We always see the same side of the Moon, the near side. The side of the Moon we cannot see is called the far side.

The Moon's path around Earth

Fun Fact

Daylight on the Moon lasts for two weeks. Could you stay awake for two weeks?

Why does the Moon seem to change shape?

The Sun always shines on half of the Moon. When the near side is in sunlight, we see a full Moon. When the far side is in sunlight, we see no Moon at all. Then it is called the new Moon. In the times between the full Moon and new Moon, we see different amounts of the Moon.

Full Moon

New Moon

How far away is the Moon?

Imagine going all the way around Earth TEN times. That is about how far the Moon is from Earth. Spaceships can get to the Moon in just three days. That is because they travel very fast.

How much would you weigh on the Moon?

The Moon has less gravity than Earth. Less gravity means there is less force pulling you down. If you weigh 60 pounds on Earth, you would weigh only 10 pounds on the Moon.

Have people visited the Moon?

Something amazing happened in 1969. Neil Armstrong and Buzz Aldrin became the FIRST people to walk on the Moon! Ten more American astronauts also visited the Moon during the next three years.

This small Moon spacecraft carried Neil Armstrong and Buzz Aldrin to the Moon.

Fun Fact

America plans to send more astronauts to the Moon in the future. Maybe you could be one of them!

Buzz Aldrin steps onto the Moon.

Is there air on the Moon?

No. When the Moon formed, it was so hot that the air and water boiled away. Astronauts on the Moon have to wear space suits. The suits have air in them for the astronauts to breathe.

Fun Fact

Mountains on the Moon have no snow. You might be able t[o] ski on them anyway because Moon dust is very slippery.

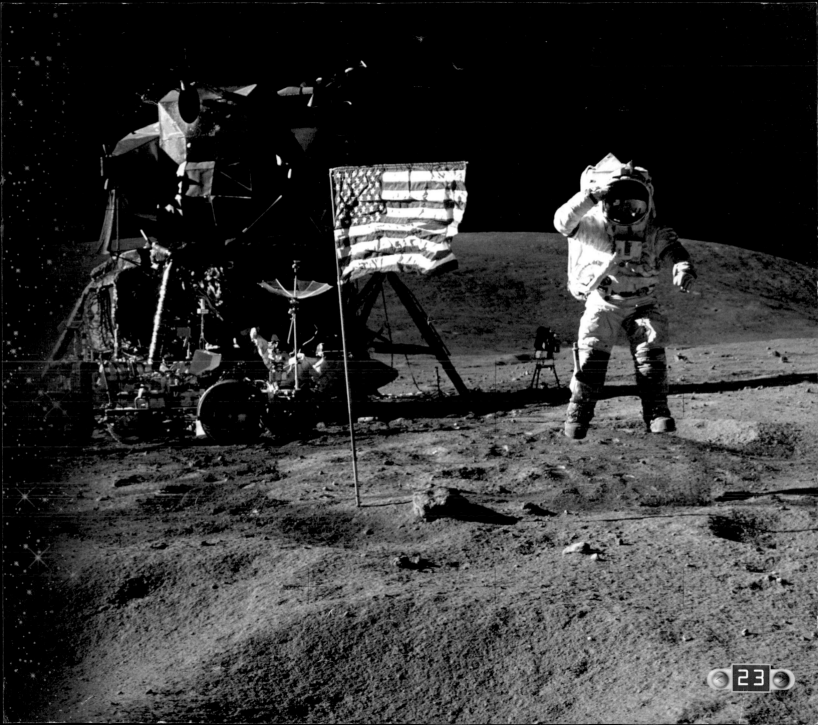

Is there sound on the Moon?

Sound travels on air. Because there is no air on the Moon, there is no sound. The Moon is very quiet. Astronauts on the Moon talked to each other on their space suit radios.

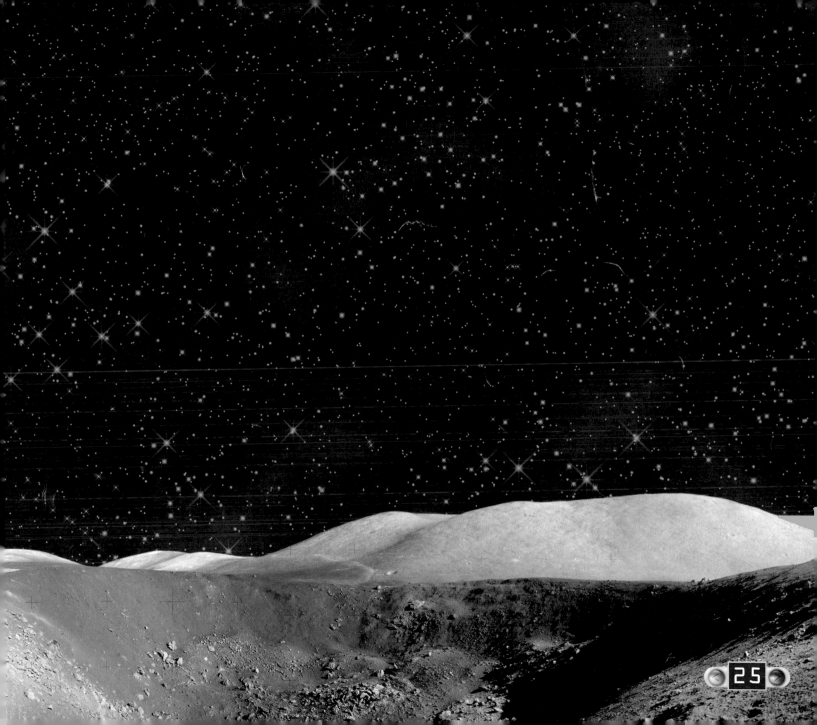

What did the astronauts bring back from the Moon?

They brought back more than 800 pounds of Moon rocks. The rocks were taken to Houston, Texas. They are stored in special boxes. Scientists have been studying the rocks for years. They look for clues that will tell them more about the Moon.

Fun Fact

Earth rocks and Moon rocks look the same. Both are hard and dry, but there is a little bit of water in Earth rocks. There is no water in Moon rocks.

27

What makes the dark spots on the Moon?

The Moon used to have big volcanoes.

Rivers of lava ran out of the volcanoes.

The lava flowed into low spots on the Moon.

The dark places you see on the Moon are really lakes of hard lava.

Who studies the Moon?

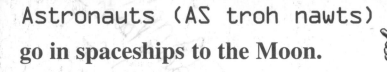

Astronauts (AS troh nawts)
go in spaceships to the Moon.

Geologists (jee AH loh jists)
study Moon rocks.

Aerospace Engineers
(AIR oh space en jih NEERZ)
make spaceships that go to the Moon.

Mission Controllers
(mih shun cun TROH lurz)
guide the spaceships to the Moon.

Books

Adamson, Thomas K. *The Moon*. Mankato, Minn.: Capstone Press, 2007.

Aldrin, Buzz. *Reaching for the Moon*. New York: Harper Collins, 2005.

Murphy, Patricia J. *Exploring Space with an Astronaut*. Berkeley Heights, N.J.: Enslow Publishers, Inc., 2004.

Web Sites

NASA. The Apollo Program.
<http://www.nasm.si.edu/collections/imagery/apollo/apollo.htm>

NASA. Star Child.
<http://starchild.gsfc.nasa.gov/docs/StarChild/StarChild.html>

INDEX

To Kate, our shining star

Enslow Elementary, an imprint of Enslow Publishers, Inc.

Enslow Elementary® is a registered trademark of Enslow Publishers, Inc.

Library of Congress Cataloging-in-Publication Data

Bredeson, Carmen.
    What is the moon? / Carmen Bredeson.
        p. cm. — (I like space!)
    Summary: "Introduces early readers to subjects about space in Q&A format"—Provided by publisher.
    Includes bibliographical references and index.
    ISBN-13: 978-0-7660-2946-0
    ISBN-10: 0-7660-2946-8
    1. Moon—Juvenile literature. I. Title.
    QB582.B749 2008
    523.3–dc22   2007002744

Printed in the United States of America

10 9 8 7 6 5 4 3 2 1

To Our Readers: We have done our best to make sure all Internet Addresses in this book were active and appropriate when we went to press. However, the author and the publisher have no control over and assume no liability for the material available on those Internet sites or on other Web sites they may link to. Any comments or suggestions can be sent by e-mail to comments@enslow.com or to the address on the back cover.

Cover Photograph: Courtesy NASA/JPL-Caltech

Illustration Credits: Carl M. Feryok (astronauts); © 2007 by Stephen Rountree (www.rountreegraphics.com), pp. 6-7, 12-13, 18, 19;

Photo Credits: Copyright António Cidadão, p. 15; Courtesy NASA/JPL-Caltech, pp. 1, 5, 9 (Moon), 11; David Nunuk/Photo Researchers, Inc., p. 29; © moonpans.com, pp. 24–25; NASA, pp. 2 (astronaut), 9 (Earth), 17; NASA Charles M. Duke, Jr., p. 23; NASA Johnson Space Center, p. 27; NASA Kennedy Space Center, p. 20; NASA Marshall Space Flight Center, p. 21; Shutterstock, blue starfield background and p. 2 (lava).

Series Literacy Consultant:
Allan A. De Fina, Ph.D.
Past President of the New Jersey Reading Association
Chairperson, Department of Literacy Education
New Jersey City University, Jersey City, New Jersey

Series Science Consultant:
Marianne J. Dyson
Former NASA Flight Controller
Science Writer
www.mdyson.com

Enslow Elementary
an imprint of
Enslow Publishers, Inc.
40 Industrial Road
Box 398
Berkeley Heights, NJ 07922
USA
http://www.enslow.com